COLOUR US BACK
FROM EXTINCTION

...

A colouring book of endangered animals

ELLE SMITH

COLOUR US BACK FROM EXTINCTION

The information contained in 'Colour Us Back from Extinction', and its components, is meant to serve for information purposes only, as researched by the author.

The author has made all reasonable efforts to provide current and accurate information for the readers of this book. The author and associates will not be held liable for any errors, unintentional or otherwise, or omissions that may be found.

The material in this book may include information from third parties. Third party materials include opinions expressed by their owners, and as such the author of this book does not assume responsibility or accept any liability for third party material or opinions.

Whether because of the progression of the Internet, or the unforeseen changes in company policy and editorial submission guidelines, what is stated as a fact at the time of this writing may become outdated or inapplicable later.

Published 2017 by Inspired By Elle (Publishing), United Kingdom
www.inspiredbyelle.com

TABLE OF CONTENTS

INTRODUCTION

As human beings, part of the reason we toil is to leave something behind for posterity. We are aware that we will not live forever, and that when we are gone, there will be others just like us, in our place.

Other animals – even though they may not be aware on a human level – should still be here through their offspring in years to come but sadly that privilege does not extend to all of them. Some of them are extinct. Others are now endangered and can even be termed "rare animals".

These animals facing extinction are in a peculiar position by no fault of their own; and as custodians of this great world we live in, there is a moral responsibility for us, as humans, to take steps to ensure that these animals do not ultimately become extinct. There have already been multiple cases of animals becoming extinct throughout history and it would be unfortunate to allow such situations to recur.

You may be asking yourself what stake you have in the matter beyond this "moral responsibility", and beyond the fact that some of these animals are beautiful to look at. The honest answer is that these animals facing extinction affect us, through their natural connection to the earth's ecosystems.

It is a fact, that all plant and animal (including human) life are interconnected, as part of one large and complex ecosystem, that includes the earth's lands and waters, and which sustains the planet. The loss of any of these components – like a single species of plant or animal – is enough to damage the ecosystem or one of its sub-ecosystems, sometimes irreparably. Ecosystems, with their chain of connected components, are the reason why our planet has such resources as breathable air, clean water, fertile soil, mineral resources and others.

The reasons for the depletion of animal numbers to the point of being endangered are many and include:

a) Habitat fragmentation

b) Pollution

c) War

d) Hunting and poaching for the production of luxury goods.

e) Climate change

f) Invasive species

g) Starvation

Of the reasons mentioned above, the majority are overwhelmingly human-induced causes. According to the World Wildlife Fund ("WWF"), the natural rate of extinction has multiplied by 100 to 1000 times, due to what it terms "destructive human activities".

We must, if for no other reason than our direct and indirect involvement in the endangering of multiple species, consider getting rare animals out of the fix they are in, and back to thriving numbers.

The danger of animals going extinct, and the potential problem for our ecosystem, is a threat acknowledged by important institutions such as world governments and research bodies. An example of this acknowledgment and subsequent action is the Endangered Species Act ("ESA") passed by the United States Congress in 1973. The act recognizes that, both endangered and threatened plants or animals are of great esthetic, ecological, educational, historical, recreational and scientific value to the Nation and its people.

The ESA states its purpose as a mission to "protect and recover imperiled species, and the ecosystems upon which they depend." Both the U.S. Fish and Wildlife Service, and the National Marine Fisheries Service ("NMFS") of the Commerce Department, administer the ESA.

It is also recognized that within the UK, several species of wildlife are under heavy threat of being endangered, and need to be protected by conservation action. The United Kingdom Biodiversity Action Plan ("UK BAP") created a list of key priority species between 1995 and 1999.

The two-year review of the UK BAP processes and priorities in 2005, gave rise to an increase of the priority species list, from the original number of less than 600 to 1150. Presently, much of the work done by the UK BAP is carried on by its successor, the "UK Post-2010 Biodiversity Framework", which was formed in 2012.

Some of the specific acts and legislation protecting wildlife in the UK include:
- The Wildlife & Countryside Act 1981,
- Protection of Animals (Amendment) Act 1988,
- The Conservation of Habitats and Species Regulation 2010.

Other countries have also taken steps over the years to combat the issue of rare animals, but this might not be enough if we don't take up the cause on a personal level.

In the following pages, we shall take a look at ten endangered animals, including facts about them, and then view the beautiful drawings to be coloured in.

1. SAND CAT

•••

DESCRIPTION

The sand cat, also known as the 'sand dune cat', is a feline creature that makes its habitat in the desert. It is able to exist, in both sandy and stony desert, and as such is found in the North African, Middle Eastern and Asian deserts.

The sand cat's fur is a pale sandy colour, which is very fitting for its desert surroundings. The patterns of its body markings vary from animal to animal, with some having spots and stripes, some faintly spotted, and some having neither spots nor stripes. The most common of markings is a black tip on the tail, and two or three dark rings towards the bottom of the tail.

While the head and back are sandy brown, the sand cat's lower face, chin, throat and whole of its underbelly, are white.

This desert cat has triangular ears with very wide ear canals that give it exceptional hearing. To protect its ears from getting filled with sand and other foreign objects, the inner parts grow very long, white, closely spaced hairs. It also has very long, white whiskers on its face.

Sand Cat

FUN FACTS

- **The sand cat was first encountered by scientists on an expedition into the Northern Algerian Sahara.** The sand cat is named after Jean Auguste Margueritte, the leader of this expedition.

- **The sand cat is the only cat in the world that lives in the desert.** It's very thick fur extends to its feet, allowing it to walk on the hot sands of the desert. Its large ears cool this cat down, and therefore make it very well adapted to the desert temperature.

- **The sand cat is too wild to be kept as a pet.** Although it is a small animal and looks a lot like a domestic cat, the sand cat is a fierce predator. It hunts snakes; hikes for miles, and can go without water for days.

- **The sand cat is a loner.** Like some other wild cats, sand cats are not big fans of living in groups. They are very solitary and in fact, the only time they actively associate with other animals of their kind is during mating season.

- **The sand cat doesn't have large litters.** The sand cat does not give birth to a large number of young ones. The average number is about four kittens per litter.

- **The sand cat is able to meow just like a domestic cat and still bark like a dog!** The sand cat is able to make more than a few types of calls including meows – which are expected – and barks – which are not!

- **The sand cat is a very fast animal.** The sand cat runs along at very fast speeds for its size, capable of reaching speeds of 25mph (40kph). Its powerful hind legs enable it to cover ground quickly over the desert and also help tremendously during hunting.

- **The sand cat is very good at digging.** This feline has mastered the art of digging and makes multiple burrows in which it lives. Some of the animals consumed by the sand cat live in burrows, which of course, this feline wastes no time in digging out.

- **The sand cat is very difficult to track.** Apart from the undersides of its small paws having thick fur as protection from the burning sand, the sand cat also has very long hairs that grow between its toes. The combination of these "foot pads" and long toe hairs make the cat's tracks very faint, and therefore very difficult to spot and follow.

2. RED SQUIRREL

• • •

DESCRIPTION

The Red squirrel, otherwise known as the "Eurasian Red squirrel" is a particular species of tree squirrel common throughout Europe and Asia. This squirrel is usually no more than 23cm in length with a mass of about 250 to 300g. The Red squirrel does not exhibit dimorphism, with the male and female having the same length and weight.

This squirrel has a long tail, which helps in balancing as it runs along tree branches. Although it is known as the "Red" squirrel, the colour of its coat varies considerably according to location and time of year. It is not unusual to see red squirrels sporting different coat hues from red to black. In Britain, the most common coat colour is red. However, in other parts of Europe and Asia, squirrels with different coat colours cohabit, causing scientists to liken the coat colours to hair colour as per human populations.

While the fur coat colours might differ, regardless of the location or time of year, the underbelly of the Red squirrel is constant; a creamy-white colour. The Red squirrel is known to shed its coat twice a year. It loses its summer coat – which is thinner – for a thicker, winter coat at some point between August and November.

Red Squirrel

Fun Facts

- **The Red squirrel is an omnivorous rodent.** The Red squirrel eats a wide range of foods and is not known to be selective of its meals. They eat buds, flowers, seeds, shoots, berries, nuts and fruits of many trees. They also eat fungi, many insects and even eat birds' eggs from time to time.

- **The Red squirrel is ambidextrous.** The Red squirrel isn't known to particularly favour any of its hands over the other. When eating or looking for food, it can use either its right hand or its left to complete the task.

- **The Red squirrel's number of digits differs from fore limb to hind limb.** The number of digits on the fore limbs is usually consistent with the number on the hind limbs for humans and many other animals. The Red squirrel however, does not follow this pattern - it has four fingers and five toes!

- **The Red Squirrel loves to build nests.** The Red squirrel is always building and it makes nests very high up in the trees, in which it rests and sleeps. The nests it builds are made of leaves, twigs and moss, and they are called "dreys".

- **The Red squirrel's pregnancy term is quite short.** The female red squirrel carries her young for just over a month – about 40 days – before giving birth. A young Red squirrel is called a "kitten".

- **The Red squirrel is a very lightweight animal.** One red squirrel weighs usually no more than 300g, and this is about the same weight, as four bars of Mars chocolate.

- **The Red squirrel does not hibernate.** Contrary to popular belief, the Red squirrel does not hibernate at all. It simply becomes less active during bad weather and may become reclusive during winter. This disappearing act during winter may have contributed to the myth of squirrels hibernating.

- **The Red squirrel can hang upside down.** In a manner similar to bats, the Red squirrel is perfectly comfortable hanging upside down. It has very sharp claws that allow it to dig deeply into tree barks to get a good grip. There is one more body part that is perhaps more important for hanging upside down: its ankles. The Red squirrel's ankles do not lock and point in one direction, instead they swivel around which allows it to rotate its feet by 180 degrees. This is the secret of the upside-down squirrel.

- **The Red squirrel is a good swimmer.** It may not do it very frequently, but the Red squirrel can actually swim. It is not known if this is an act of recreation or something else, however this squirrel can wade out a good number of metres into a sizeable water body, and even float properly.

3. SNOW LEOPARD

●●●

DESCRIPTION

The snow leopard is a large cat found in mountainous areas of Central and South Asia. It favours alpine and subalpine zones at elevations of 10,000 to 15,000 ft. In the northernmost parts of the areas where they are found, they can be found at much lower elevations.

The snow leopard is one of the smallest of the big cats. It has short legs and a very long tail. To help it survive in the harsh, snowy ranges it occupies, it possesses long thick fur. The colour of this fur ranges from grey to yellow. The snow leopard has dark-coloured rosettes or spots on its body with corresponding spots of the same colour on its head. The spots continue on the legs and tail, and get bigger as they go further down.

The thick fur enables it to minimize heat loss along with the small, rounded ears. Its long tail is very flexible, which helps it maintain balance as it leaps from rock to rock.

The snow leopard has very large nasal cavities, which are very essential because it needs to breathe the thin, cold air of its surroundings.

Snow Leopard

Fun Facts

- **The snow leopard can be seen from Siberia all the way to the Tibetan Plateau.** They particularly like these areas because of the cliffs and ravines. These vantage points provide them an unbeatable view of prey and allow them to sneak up on them.

- **The snow leopard uses its large tail as a blanket while it sleeps.** The snow leopard's long, large tail is very thick with fur on the outside and fat on the inside. So while sleeping, it curls the tail all the way to its face, to provide warmth as it sleeps in the blistering cold.

- **The snow leopard's huge paws act like snowshoes.** The snow can get to several feet deep, in the areas where the snow leopard lives. The snow leopard has huge, chunky paws, which act like snowshoes, using their width to allow the cat to move efficiently, and thus to never get stuck. Their paw pads also have extra linings of fur, which provide traction and prevent them from slipping on icy surfaces.

- **The snow leopard cannot roar.** This big cat is unlike its cousins, the lion and the tiger, in one significant way – it cannot roar. It's not exactly clear why it does not have this ability, but is most likely due to its larynx structure, which does not have certain components present in lions and tigers. The snow leopard communicates with other sounds including growls, hisses, wails and chuffs.

- **The snow leopard avoids fighting with man.** This big cat is a great hunter and is certainly very carnivorous, but when it comes to man, it tends to walk away every single time. While lions and tigers are quick to get into violent confrontations with man, the snow leopard does the exact opposite. In fact, if a human interrupts a snow leopard during a feeding session, its natural reaction will be to run away, as opposed to standing its ground and defending its food.

- **The snow leopard is crepuscular.** This simply means that it is active during dawn and dusk. Its hours of activity in a day are very few. The snow leopard has therefore earned a reputation of being a shy, reclusive animal; especially as its snow-camouflaged fur makes it difficult to spot.

- **The snow leopard eats a significant amount of vegetation.** Although the snow leopard is an accomplished hunter, which can kill animals up to four times its weight. It is also a very unusual cat, in that eats a lot of grass and twigs.

4. PILEATED GIBBON

●●●

DESCRIPTION

The pileated gibbon is a distinctive primate that is found naturally in just three countries of the world: Cambodia, Laos and Thailand.

Even from afar, it is very easy to differentiate the male pileated gibbon from the female. The male possesses predominantly black fur with its hands, feet and brow bands as the only white parts. The female, on the other hand, has silvery-grey fur, with a black head and black belly. A white, shaggy hair ring around the sides of the head is a feature common to both the male and the female.

The young pileated gibbon, whether male or female, is similar in colour to the adult female and doesn't begin to change its colour to a darker hue until it begins to approach adulthood.

This ape is similar in body structure to other gibbons, possessing a slender body with long forearms and no tail at all. It primarily moves by swinging itself effortlessly from branch to branch but when necessary, the pileated gibbon can move some distance on foot. It is mostly a frugivore, living on fruits with very high sugar content. But when necessary, it can also supplement its diet with vegetation. It performs most of its actions during the day and by evening, it retires to a tall tree to rest and prepare for the night.

Pileated Gibbon

Fun Facts

- **The pileated gibbon has a powerful swing.** This ape has very strong hands that carry its body effortlessly. Its swing is so strong that it can throw itself from one tree to another over space of more than nine metres.

- **The pileated gibbon is monogamous.** This ape is known for its ability to stick to one partner for the duration of its lifespan.

- **The pileated gibbon makes duets.** Yes, the pileated gibbon actually makes "musical" duets, which are complex and beautiful. A male and female within their monogamous pair make these duets. With the use of throat sacs under their chin, they are able to enhance the calls they make during the duet. The female starts the duet with a very loud and distinctive call made up of rich, rising notes that last for about 18 seconds. The male joins in with a call that is not as loud, consisting of abrupt notes and a trill. These duets are believed to reinforce the bonds between a breeding pair. They are also used to mark out the territory of the pair, along with threats and displays.

5. GALAPAGOS PENGUIN

•••

DESCRIPTION

The Galapagos penguin, from its name, is a penguin native to the Galapagos Islands. It is able to live in the tropical climate of these islands because of two factors. Firstly, the cool temperatures caused by the Humboldt Current, and secondly the cool water from great depths, which is carried up by the Cromwell Current.

This penguin is the only one in the world that lives north of the equator and is a member of the banded penguins, although those other species all live mostly in South America and the coasts of Africa. The Galapagos penguin is one of the smallest of the penguin species, and weighs in at just about 2.5 kg.

All penguins are generally known to be black and white, but the Galapagos penguin can be identified by its specific markings. Its head is mainly black with a white border that runs behind the eye around the ear-coverts and chin. This white border extends further to the throat. There are two black bands that run across the white breast, and one of them goes down the flanks to the thighs of the bird. The young Galapagos penguin is different in colour from the adult, with a dark head, grey sides and no breast band.

Galapagos Penguin

Fun Facts

- **The Galapagos penguin sleeps in burrows.** When it is time to rest, the Galapagos penguin resorts to burrows in the solid ground.

- **The Galapagos penguin is very sedentary.** This bird is not an explorer and will not go anywhere, unless absolutely necessary. It sleeps on land and spends time on water to feed and regulate its temperature; making shifts to and fro as necessary. It always stays near its colony, and does not attempt to go more than 3 miles away.

- **The Galapagos penguin is a diver.** Although it is brought food by water currents, this bird sometimes dives into water to hunt. On the average, it dives to depths of 26ft, however there have been recorded incidents of dives to around 180ft.

- **The Galapagos penguin moults up to twice a year.** The Galapagos penguin has been known to experience moulting twice a year, even though once a year is not abnormal. The pre-moulting process begins two to four weeks before the main moult, and during this time, the penguin adds weight by a few grammes. The main moulting takes place over an average of 13 days and during this period, the bird can lose up to 40% of its total body mass.

- **The Galapagos penguin hunts from below.** The Galapagos penguin's diet consists of small fish – for example sardines, anchovies, mullets, and tiny crustaceans. One of its hunting techniques is to submerge itself in water, and watch from below as fish swim above it. It then rises quickly and grabs a meal for itself.

- **The Galapagos penguin has weird physical features, compared to other penguins.** This bird has some strange features indeed, including longer, more slender bills. Another weird feature is the presence of patches of bare skin around its eyes and also at the base of the bill.

- **The Galapagos penguin has unique techniques for regulating its body temperature.** This bird is not a fan of too much heat and remains by the water as much as possible to cool itself down. When on land, it stands with its flippers outstretched, to enable the loss of excess heat by radiation. Equally when it walks, it does so slightly hunched, to keep its feet in the shade of its flippers. The Galapagos penguin also pants to cool itself; with the mouth open, it makes use of evaporation to cool down its throat and airways. The young penguin chicks are not left out from this, as they develop brown feathers about 30 days after they hatch, to provide protection from the harsh sun.

- **The male and female Galapagos penguins take turn to incubate eggs.** The female penguin lays her eggs in deep crevices in the rocks, to avoid the hot sun from overheating them. The process of incubation lasts for about 40 days, with both the male and female Galapagos penguin taking an active part in the process. While one partner is with the egg, the other might be away for days at a time, feeding. The couples take feeding very seriously, and if there is a scarcity of food while incubating, they might abandon the nest with their eggs.

- **The Galapagos penguin is the least noisy of all the penguins.** The calls and vocalizations made by this bird are determined by the purpose of said calls for example, hunting or coordination. The sounds are similar to donkey brays and so the Galapagos penguin has earned the nickname, "The jackass penguin".

6. GIANT PANDA

•••

DESCRIPTION

The Giant panda is a bear natural to South Central Asia, and is also known as the "panda bear" or simply "panda". It is mostly called the Giant panda, when the need arises to differentiate it from the red panda, a mammal of another family.

The Giant panda has a large, roundish body typical of bears, which is covered with luxuriant black and white fur. The distribution of the black and white is as follows: there is black fur on the animal's eye patches, eyes, muzzle, shoulders, arms and legs; while the remaining parts of its body are covered in white fur. It is unclear why the panda has such a distinct colouring. The belief is that they developed this coat, to effectively camouflage themselves against their snowy, rocky and shady habitat.

The adult panda can grow to as much as 6ft tall with an average weight of about 110kg. However, some pandas can weigh up to 150kg. The giant panda's large paw consists of six fingers and one thumb, which is actually a modified sesamoid bone. This "thumb" helps it to properly hold its food – mostly bamboo – while it eats.

Giant Panda

Fun Facts

- **The Giant panda prefers to be alone.** The panda is quite the solitary animal and likes to roam about and eat mostly by itself. Each adult defines its territory and prefers to stay there on its own. This attitude is especially worse with females who will not tolerate another female hanging around her range. The Giant panda is most social during breeding season. During this period, any pandas close together will gather around each other but after the mating is done, the male will leave the female alone and she will raise the cub.

- **The Giant panda does not rely heavily on visual memory.** The panda does not depend on seeing, recognizing and remembering for most of its actions. Instead, it depends on spatial memory, which is a cognitive process that allows for quick remembering of locations as well as the positioning of objects, kind of how we move through a dark room and avoid bumping into some objects.

- **The Giant panda can eat as much as 14kg of bamboo in a day!** The panda is classified as a carnivorous animal mostly because of its genes and digestive system, however about 99% of its diet is made up of bamboo. The panda's carnivorous digestive system struggles to digest the cellulose in bamboo efficiently, and to produce sufficient levels of energy. Therefore, the panda has to eat large volumes of bamboo in order to get sufficient nutrition. Consequently, it can eat anywhere from 10 to 14kg of bamboo every day. The low energy diet of the panda makes it stay in one place for long periods, moving around only when necessary. Some scientists think that its low-energy diet might be part of the reason it is not a very 'social' creature.

- **The Giant panda can defecate up to 40 times a day.** The panda has a short and straight digestive tract, so the large volumes of food pass through its digestion quickly. Such a rapid intake doesn't give room for efficient digestion, so the microbial digestion process in the gastrointestinal tract is limited. This makes the panda pass out waste about 40 times in a single day.

- **Panda cubs are very small.** The giant panda gives birth to cubs that are totally helpless. The cubs are born blind, toothless and arrive as fragile, pink newborns. The giant panda cub weighs from about 100 to 130 grammes at birth and so proportionally, is the smallest baby of all placental mammals.

7. MANDARIN DUCK

●●●

DESCRIPTION

The Mandarin duck is a perching duck originally native to East Asia. It bred naturally in great numbers in China and Japan, but their numbers have reduced drastically, due to large-scale exportation and habitat destruction. These days, the Mandarin duck is found in other parts of the world including California (U.S.A.), parts of England and Ireland. This is as a result of some individual birds escaping captivity and starting wild breeding populations. In fact, the number of Mandarin ducks in England is about seven times the number found in China.

The Mandarin duck is regarded as a medium-sized bird with a length of about 41 to 49cm. The wingspan of the bird is about 65 to 67cm.

The Mandarin duck exhibits dimorphism, as the male and female are very different. The female Mandarin duck is mostly of a grey-brown colour. It has a white eye ring and white stripe that runs backwards. There is also a small white stripe on the side of the female, and her bill is of a pale colour.

The male Mandarin duck is a striking bird and is usually described as "hard to miss". It is a brightly coloured bird, with a red bill and reddish face with a large, white crescent over the eye. Its back is covered in deep green and blue feathers, while its breast is purple with white bars running vertically. The tail feathers of the male are a bright orange and the underbelly is white.

Both the male and the female Mandarin duck have crests, but the crest on the male is more pronounced, by far. The male Mandarin duck experiences a moult after the mating season, shedding into an "eclipse plumage". During the eclipse plumage stage, the male becomes more similar to the female, yet it can still be distinguished by the following characteristics: no crest, a less-pronounced eye stripe and a yellow-orange bill.

Mandarin Duck

Fun Facts

- **The Mandarin duck is widely regarded as the world's most beautiful duck.** With the stunning plumage of the male duck clear for all to see, this title is largely uncontested. This duck is a popular choice for artists because of its stunning looks, and it is particularly favoured in Oriental art.

- **The Mandarin duck is a skilful flyer.** The Mandarin duck is only capable of limited flight, and yet performs very skilful manoeuvres. Trees pose no real obstacle threat, because it can fly through them in very agile arcs.

- **The Mandarin duck is a small bird in a small pond.** The Mandarin duck, like all ducks, is drawn to water but this particular duck does not favour large water bodies. It avoids lakes and other large bodies of open water with a passion, and would rather dive in a small, wooded pond.

- **The Mandarin duck is a serial escapee.** This duck does not enjoy captivity, and will most likely abscond from a domestic enclave even after many years have passed. The first birds imported to Britain showed this trait. The first Mandarin ducks were imported sometime in the mid-18th century. They were held captive as domestic ducks for several generations until their eventual escape in the 1930s in the county of Surrey (U.K.). They began to breed in the wild, and Surrey developed into an area with a large Mandarin duck population.

- **The Mandarin ducklings are encouraged to be acrobatic from day one!** The female Mandarin duck lays her eggs in a hole or cavity in a tree trunk. Though the male might protect her and the eggs, he does not incubate the eggs himself and always leaves before the eggs finally hatch. After they hatch, the mother duck flies to the ground and encourages her ducklings to jump to the ground. They do and almost always land successfully and without injuries due to their very light weight and ample feathers. The moment they land on the ground, their mother leads them straight to a body of water.

- **The Mandarin duck is regarded as a symbol of fidelity even though it really isn't faithful.** The Mandarin Duck is seen as symbol of fidelity, in its native home of China. It is an old Chinese tradition to present a bride with a pair of Mandarin ducks. In reality, Mandarin ducks are not faithful in their relationships. They, like most ducks, only pair for the approaching mating season. They disengage thereafter, and form new pairs with the next mating season.

8. RING-TAILED LEMUR OF MADAGASCAR

●●●

DESCRIPTION

The ring-tailed lemur is a very social primate native to Madagascar. It is also by far, the most popular of all the lemurs. It shares some striking characteristics with the domestic cat. It has a white and black ring-tailed pattern, which is reflective of the cat and amazingly, the lemur also purrs.

Of all the members of the lemur family, the ring-tailed is the most terrestrial, although it also spends time in the trees. It is one of the largest lemurs, weighing in at around 2kg.

The ring-tailed lemur possesses thick fur that is so strong, that it can actually clog electric clippers.

Ring~Tailed Lemur

Fun Facts

- **The word "lemur" comes from the French word for "spirit" or "ghost."** This is fitting, as the ring-tailed lemur indeed has a striking resemblance to something out of a ghost story.

- **The ring-tailed lemur loves to sunbathe.** It sunbathes extensively, especially its underside, and performs all of its activities during the sunshine. Scientists call animals that behave in this manner "diurnal". This word shows the ring-tailed lemur to be the exact opposite of nocturnal.

- **The popular movie, *Madagascar,* which was set in Madagascar, has the lemur as its main character.** The island of Madagascar is actually the only place in the world, where the lemur lives in the wild.

- **Ring-tailed lemurs can survive extreme conditions.** Whether cold or hot, the lemur will find a way to survive, and this is why it is the most populous primate in Madagascar. This species of the lemur family is so resilient and productive in captivity, that it is now found almost everywhere in the world. Strangely, the ring-tailed lemur has seen a sharp decline in numbers, making it an endangered species.

- **The Ring-tailed lemur is quite the smart animal.** It understands basic arithmetic operations, can do things in sequence, and can choose tools based on functionality. It can do all this despite its brain being quite small.

- **The Ring-tailed lemur battles by way of stink fights.** Have you ever been in a stink fight? The lemur probably invented this tactic. They secrete stinky scents from their wrist glands, smearing this on their tails and then waft it on their opponents during mating fights. It is of course, the males who exhibit this behaviour. The females also have secretions but they use these to mark territories, not to engage in stink battles.

- **The Ring-tailed lemur is believed to hold souls.** Many traditional natives of the island of Madagascar believe that the lemurs harbour the souls of their ancestors. This belief may have arisen, in part, because the lemur uses varied vocalizations to communicate. These vocalizations, in local folklore, are said to be human voices in animal skin.

- **The Ring-tailed lemur has a lifespan of about 15 years.** The Ring-tailed lemur lives about 12-15 years in the wild, if it is not eaten by one of the numerous predators that dwell with them on the Island.

9. NEWFOUNDLAND PINE MARTEN

●●●

DESCRIPTION

This Newfoundland pine marten is a small mammal found only in Newfoundland, Canada. This area-specific existence accounts for its name but there is another reason it is named so, with "Newfoundland" as a prefix. This is to differentiate it from its American cousin, the American marten.

The Newfoundland pine marten is a bit bigger than its American cousin, and can be easily distinguished by its dark brown fur, and the presence of an orange or yellow patch on the throat. It loves to hang around old forest trees that have been around for 60 to 80 years, because they provide the kinds of foods it loves, such as insects and smaller mammals.

The Newfoundland pine marten is an omnivore by nature and as such, is not picky over its meals. It regularly consumes a healthy balanced diet of vegetables, along with some solid meat, eggs and berries.

The Newfoundland pine marten naturally lives for about 8 to 10 years. However, when it is taken away from the wild and cared for, it can live for up to 15 years.

The Newfoundland pine marten prefers its own company until it's time to mate, which is usually during mid-summer.

The Newfoundland pine marten is a victim of human trapping because of its beautiful fur – a problem that also affects its cousins, the mink and the weasel. It gets worse as the marten sometimes fall into traps that were not even set for them.

Newfoundland Pine Marten

Fun Facts

- **It is usually the female Newfoundland pine marten who initiates mating proceedings.** Just like the weasel, the marten sprays its scent on the ground and on trees to attract its partner.

- **The Newfoundland pine marten gives birth to its young underground.** The female pine marten heads underground when it's time to give birth. The most likely explanation is, that she is better able to protect her little ones from predators whilst underground. The baby marten is usually deaf and blind at birth, and they remain underground, under "Witness Protection", for a period of about 42 days.

- **The Newfoundland pine marten is very polygamous.** This marten does not care about sharing, during mating, or indeed breeding seasons. The average marten is known to have several partners, and therefore produces offspring in large numbers. This could offer an explanation, as to how the species has been able to escape its "critically endangered" status, and is now considered only as being "threatened".

- **The Newfoundland pine marten has a great number of predators.** In the wild, there is a wide range of predators that find the Newfoundland pine marten very delicious and hunt it aggressively. Some of them are the lynx, the great horned owl, the hawk and the red fox.

10. AMUR LEOPARD

• • •

DESCRIPTION

The Amur leopard is a species of leopard that is only found in some parts of Russia and China. The major habitat of this leopard is around the Amur River, and it is from this river, that the leopard derives its name.

It varies from other leopards through its thick coat of spotted fur, which is known to be very divergent in pattern. The soft coat with long dense hair changes slightly with the time of the year. It varies from light yellow to yellowish-red, or a golden or rusty reddish-yellow, during the winter. Whereas, it takes on a brighter yellowish hue in the summer.

The Amur leopard has a slightly more unique colouration than its other cousins, with larger rosettes and a more vibrant colour. The Amur leopard is widely considered as the most beautiful leopard of the species. This label has not always had positive ramifications. The leopard is heavily desired, and as a consequence 'hunted', by fur traders and poachers for its beautiful fur.

The Amur leopard is one of the small leopards. The males are slightly heavier than the females at 32 to 47kg while the females weigh about 25 to 40kg.

The Amur leopard possesses long limbs, which are adept at walking smoothly through very deep snow. They are so endangered that they presently exist in only a small area between the China-Russia borders, which has an area of about 2500km^2.

It takes about 2 to 3 years before a female Amur leopard becomes ready to become a mother. She can upon maturity breed cubs for as long as 10 to 15 years. The male cub tends to be the explorer of the species. Males are so keen for independence that they tend to leave home before their second birthday. Usually, only the weaker males stay around where they were raised, for beyond the first two years.

An Amur leopard can live for up to 15 years in the wild. However, in captivity, it is possible for them to live as long as 21 years.

One of the Amur leopard's biggest problems is a lack of genetic diversity. This causes it to have a high rate of inbreeding and therefore weakens the line of the leopards. This is one of the reasons the Amur leopard is an endangered species.

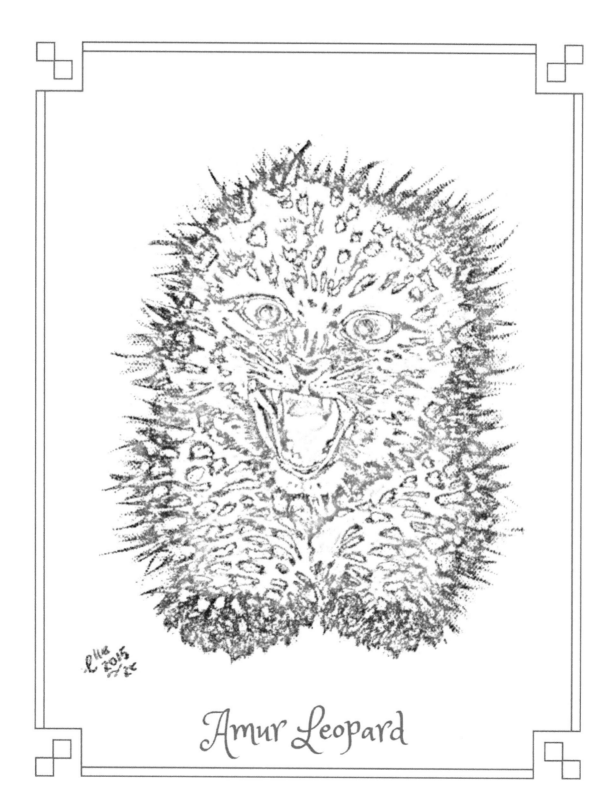

Amur Leopard

Fun Facts

- **The Amur leopard is a great leaper.** This leopard can leap, on an average, more than 19ft far and 10ft high.

- **The Amur leopard is crepuscular.** The Amur leopard is mostly active between dusk and dawn. This leopard is very comfortable lying in a cave and sleeping, when it is not actively hunting.

- **The Amur leopard is extremely territorial.** This leopard is so particular about its privacy that it marks its territory for spaces as much as 100km^2. It really does not tolerate encroachment of its personal space by other leopards. However, it may share hunting trails and other natural amenities, including water, with others.

- **The Amur leopard is strictly carnivorous.** This leopard eats nothing else but meat, and is a true member of the carnivorous family. The Amur leopard has a strong preference for fresh deer meat, but does not mind the tasty meat of other animals such as the moose, wild pig, hare and fowl.

A NOTE FROM THE AUTHOR:
WHY I PAINT ENDANGERED ANIMALS

•••

I think that the earth is an absolutely gorgeous planet. Everything on it is purposeful and beautiful, and that's only part of the appeal. While I appreciate the greatness of Earth on a daily basis, I have also come to appreciate that our handling and management of the planet could be much better.

Whether out of ignorance, or a sheer contempt for the place we all call home, we have all become culprits in the gradual degradation of Earth. Whether as heavy polluters like industry owners, or light polluters like car owners and spray users, or just as regular people who burn stuff or don't recycle; we have all contributed to the problem Earth presently faces.

You might not believe in the effects of pollution or the existence of global warming but look around you, their effects are real. If you ask the folk who came before you or look at pictures from decades ago – both of the Earth from space and even our major cities – you'll see the glaring truth: our planet is not getting better, it's getting worse.

If you do realize it, then you can begin to consciously do the right thing for Earth. Live green and involve your local communities for it will be worth it in the end.

I personally believe that some of us are aware of Earth's problems, but instead choose to ignore the animals the planet loses yearly. The truth is they're not just wild, irrelevant animals we can do without; they're active members of our great ecosystem and residents of Earth in their own right. We have a responsibility towards them and ourselves to keep them alive. If you do not have compassion for them, then at least have some for yourself.

It's becoming obvious, as the days pass, that a destroyed ecosystem will destroy us. If it doesn't come in our time, then it will come in that of our children, unless we begin to stem the tide.

I try to create awareness for endangered animals by making oil paintings of them. A good number of these paintings are also available as giclée prints that can be given as gifts to remind us of the beautiful animals we are losing.

If you want to take a look at my paintings, kindly log on to the following page:

https://www.inspiredbyelle.com/collections/animals

I also have a YouTube channel that would be of great interest to you. I encourage you to stop by and put your hands in mine as we try to save the planet.

https://www.youtube.com/channel/UCJRn5QmZZ3vAYJ9Xv0dR5_A

Kindest,

Elle Smith

www.inspiredbyelle.com

Lightning Source UK Ltd.
Milton Keynes UK
UKHW050851211022
410789UK00004B/42